CHARTING YOUR GOALS

CHARTING YOUR GOALS

PERSONAL LIFE-GOALS PLANNER

SELF-DIRECTED EXERCISES THAT WILL HELP YOU ACHIEVE
YOUR PERSONAL AND BUSINESS OBJECTIVES IN THE AREAS
OF CAREER, HEALTH, RELATIONSHIPS, FINANCES,
PERSONAL GROWTH, AND VALUES CLARIFICATION

DAN DAHL AND RANDOLPH SYKES

PERENNIAL LIBRARY

HARPER & ROW, PUBLISHERS, NEW YORK
CAMBRIDGE, PHILADELPHIA, SAN FRANCISCO, LONDON
MEXICO CITY, SÃO PAULO, SINGAPORE, SYDNEY

A spiral-bound edition of *Charting Your Goals* was published in 1987 by Dolphin Circle, Mill Valley, California.

First PERENNIAL LIBRARY edition published 1988.

Library of Congress Cataloging-in-Publication Data

Dahl, Dan.
   Charting your goals.
   1. Vocational guidance.   2. Career development.   3. Life skills.   4. Success.   5. Goal (Psychology)   I. Sykes, Randolph.   II. Title.
HF5381.D14   1988   650.1   88-45022
ISBN 0-06-096297-6 (pbk.)

      90 91 92 DT/MP 10 9 8 7 6 5 4 3 2

For information about our audio products, write us at:
Newbridge Book Clubs, 3000 Cindel Drive, Delran, NJ 08370

La'a Laka aloha

CONTENTS

PREFACE

During the Christmas season of 1978, I started the annual ritual of setting my New Year's resolutions. I anticipated the usual futile exercise of making decisions that would be abandoned well before mid-year.

In a casual conversation about my frustration at setting resolutions, my friend and co-worker Randolph Sykes outlined a formula he had developed in answer to the same concern. The techniques we discussed that day grew into *Charting Your Goals*.

The insight I gained from our conversation was that in order to work, personal goals had to be based on long-term objectives, on self-knowledge, and on the calibration of expectations and resources.

We concluded that what we needed was a program that would help us achieve our personal goals by connecting them with our daily lives.

The personal planning formula contained in this book represents a new approach to achievement. It makes use of self-directed exercises that help people identify their personal goals, their patterns of success and failure, and their expectations for the future. And, it puts that information into a workable format.

Since it was introduced in 1979, *Charting Your Goals* has been the key to achievement for many people like yourself. Its scope has recently been expanded to include personal value clarification.

I hope that *Charting Your Goals* enhances your opportunities and helps you to achieve the success in life you want.

Dan Dahl

USING THIS WORKBOOK

Charting Your Goals is a method for helping you set and achieve your goals. Your success depends on you.

In order to get maximum benefit from this workbook:

- Work at your own pace.
- Read each section thoroughly. You will be asked to do some exercises to assist your understanding of the topics discussed.
- Complete the written exercises. This is your personal workbook. You should treat it as you would any other personal and confidential material.
- Be honest with yourself. Accurate assessment of your experience is vital to making *Charting Your Goals* work for you.
- Relax. You are most able to plan for the future when you have put yourself into a relaxed frame of mind and are physically at ease.
- Commit yourself to the process. Understanding your goals—and what it will take to achieve them—requires contemplation and commitment.

PROLOGUE

HUMAN TRANSFORMATION

We are in a time of great change. Change can be a process of both disruption and renewal. It occurs at moments when existing pictures, beliefs, and values become old, outmoded, or dysfunctional. All of a sudden, events no longer seem to fit the reasonable assumptions we have traditionally used to explain them.

Feelings of uncertainty are challenging and changing some of our most fundamental assumptions about society. These feelings are transforming many of our beliefs as well as how we think about our world. They are also transforming us. We are seeing how change affects us, as well as our families, friends, neighbors, and employers. The lack of stability of both financial markets and employment outlook and the transitory nature of many relationships contribute to our experience of this transforming process.

In periods of transition, passage, crisis, or development we experience the uncertainty of future possibilities as well as our hopes and fears about what may happen to us. Being aware of and articulating our values, needs, and goals give us greater control over how these transitions affect us and enhance our ability to manage potential outcomes. When we are clear about our personal values—can articulate our needs and set reasonable goals—we gain a sense of direction and stability that may not otherwise be available to us as we face change.

Learning to manage change successfully leads us to understand more about how human beings transform themselves. Human transformation entails nothing less than clarifying values, reassessing priorities, and setting goals that foster the fulfillment of essential needs and greatest potential. Human transformation is mandatory if our society and its institutions are to survive into the 1990s and beyond.

It is important to view human transformation both in its historical context and in its current cultural manifestation. In the 1960s, there was a social awakening in the West that focused on the individual and a recognition and approval of new behavior patterns. This new social consciousness coincided with renewed interest in the religions and philosophy of the Orient. A new value system began to express itself in the establishment of acceptable alternatives to the nuclear family, traditional relationships, and conventional work habits, as well as in new approaches to problem-solving and business management.

In the 1970s, these concepts and new visions emerged into what has been termed the "personal growth movement." This era was typified by organizations, groups, and cults that promoted a greater vision of the possibilities of life and emphasized both self-esteem and the importance of personal enlightenment.

The generation emerging with its "counter-culture" vision in the 1960s entered mainstream business by the early 1980s. Persons who had experience in individual growth processes began to synthesize a well-defined set of values and to apply them on personal and professional levels.

This shift in values and ideas, coupled with the global recession and economic failure of many businesses in the 1980s and the collapse of financial markets in 1987, began to raise serious questions about the effectiveness of traditional business approaches and theories. Questions began to concentrate on the ability of business to meet the needs of employees for economic prosperity, security, and personal satisfaction while, at the same time, maintaining loyalty and improving productivity.

The means of transformation are visible in rising perspectives for directing personal potential and achievement. New avenues for linking personal and business objectives are evident in the entrepreneurial spirit that has emerged from the quest for economic advancement and self-realization.

Individuals are hoping for a way to sustain their enthusiasm and build the determination necessary to achieve their greatest potential. American business is currently searching for a methodology acceptable to its culture and uniform enough to motivate the diversity of people and systems it employs.

Charting Your Goals is such a vehicle and provides individuals and business with the opportunity for ensuring mutual success and reward.

ACKNOWL-EDGMENTS

There are many people we wish to thank for their ideas and contributions to the concept of personal life-goals planning and to the writing and publishing of this book: Our friends at Harper & Row, especially Bill Shinker and our editor Terry Karten; Reid Boates, for seeing our vision; the many friends, teachers, and scholars whose ideas have helped to change our lives and who assisted us as we developed new models of human transformation; and those who helped us bring *Charting Your Goals* into being, including Claire Dahl and Marguerite Sykes, to whom we owe eternal gratitude, Shirley Barger, Janet Hadland Davis, Allan DeForno, Elizabeth Glaze, Laurence and Cheryl Lyons, Dale and Gail McKenzie, Nancy Noll, Suzanne Simmonds, and Elizabeth Worley, who encouraged us at each step along the way.

In addition, we extend our thanks to Barbara Block, Michel Boynton, Sean Brennan, Jim Filippi, David Freidberg, Lyn Davis Genelli, Virginia Logan, Emmett Marx, Ric McGredy, Fritz Offensend, Mary and Lila Rhodes, Joe Ryan, Lenore Tuttle, Frank Wantland, and Paula Zand—each of whom helped us in some special way realize our vision; to Richard Bandler, Vic Baranco, John Bradshaw, W. Edwards Demming, Peter Drucker, Shakti Gawain, John Grindler, Oscar Ichazo, Abraham Maslow, Patanjali, Fritz Perls, Catherine Ponder, Shankara, R. G. H. Siu, and Maharishi Mahesh Yogi, who hold special places in the pantheon of great teachers; and to our fathers, Wesley Dahl and Joseph Sykes.

one
YOUR
VIEWPOINTS

In this chapter, you will have the opportunity to review your viewpoints about six areas:

- FAILURE   • SUCCESS
- POWER   • MONEY
- TIME   • PROCESS

These are key topics which affect your ability to achieve your goals. Your viewpoints about them serve as the parameters within which your success is possible.

Your viewpoints are the ways in which you look at things. A viewpoint is an attitude of the mind. For example, your attitudes about your work or your family, or what you like and do not like, or your political and social affiliations are all viewpoints.

You are not your viewpoints. You are distinct from them. You adopt viewpoints that prove to be useful for you and, as such, you are the co-designer and manager of your viewpoints about yourself, others, and the things around you.

Imagine that you have set sail and, on the horizon, you see another ship. You may think about where it is going or who the passengers are. You are an observer. Just as you can observe this other ship, you are able to look at your own viewpoints and describe your thoughts about them.

This is an important understanding because many

1

people personally identify with their viewpoints. They believe that their perspectives are true and correct and are never (or are infrequently) subject to change. They often assume that the viewpoints of others are in error or are to be treated with suspicion.

For many of you, viewpoints about who you are, or how things should or should not be, place limits on your ability to have what you want. For example, if your viewpoint is that you have an inherited weight problem, it is probable that you will be unsuccessful at controlling your weight through diet; or, if your viewpoint is that your station in life should not be better than that of your parents, you will tend to remain at or below the economic and social levels of your family.

Since viewpoints provide a useful function, they may change as new circumstances or new information renders an existing viewpoint ineffectual. Although your viewpoints may change, they tend to remain constant and operative unless you take deliberate steps to change them. Sometimes they are deeply rooted in traditional beliefs, family ties, and social values.

Understanding your viewpoints is essential if you are to have the flexibility needed to pursue a successful life-plan.

Failure and Success

All achievers face the possibility of failure. Wherever the opportunity for success exists, so does the possibility of failure.

Some persons fail and never try again. Defeated, they return to safe waters where they are no longer open to challenges. Such response to failure limits future success because it precludes additional adventures. The result of failure is not a state of existence. Failure is an act. A failure occurs at a point in time, and as the consequence of some process.

Fear of failure is the biggest obstacle to success.

The most effective of all human fears which prevent development of full potential are the fear of failure and the fear of success. Once you set sail, doubting the accuracy of your charts makes the outcome of your voyage uncertain. That is not to say you will never encounter obstacles even in well-known waters. However, as Captain of your own ship, it is important for you to compensate for unknown factors such as no wind, reefs, or rough waters. Such conditions may force you to change your course on short notice.

"Counter intentions" work in much the same way as reefs and rough waters. Counter intentions are thoughts which deny or question what you want to accomplish or attain. Counter intentions include both spoken and unspoken doubts about your purpose, your goals, or your abilities. If you doubt your ability to succeed, there is a high degree of probability that you will not be successful.

When you intend to be successful, the likelihood that you will achieve your goals improves.

Failure teaches an important truth about success: that either your stated goal was not what you really wanted or your strategy and tactics for achieving your goal were either inappropriate or ill-timed. (For more discussion of strategies and tactics, see pages 84–85.) Although you may experience temporary, or even sustained, remorse or sense of loss as the result of a failure, most often you will come to understand the lesson that **failure is success trying to be born in a bigger or better way.**

Most failures set the stage for other changes and opportunities, and ultimately, for success.

Success is not always the opposite of failure. Failures are an indication that the chemistry, motivation, or circumstances underlying your actions may be inappropriate for the goal you want. Imagine that you are mid-ocean and plagued with bad weather as well as a series of mechanical failures on board your boat. The odds that you may not reach your destination are clearly rising. If you are only able to save yourself and reach safety, do you call your voyage a "failure"? Although you did not reach your intended destination you would have surely learned some valuable lessons for your next voyage. Simply put, failure lowers your odds!

In the context of life-planning, success is the favorable outcome of an event or series of events aimed at a specific goal. Sometimes that "favorable outcome" may be exactly what was intended or desired. Other times, success may include twists and turns that you may not have anticipated but which contribute to or enhance your future opportunities. Reaching your destination safely may require you to stop at ports you had not scheduled.

Your image of what it means to be successful is the composite of your dreams, goals, and ambitions, and what you perceive it would be like to live in the best of all possible worlds, at the best of all possible times. This image—your picture of success—may change over time. It is highly dependent upon past and present circumstances for its overall character.

Whereas failure is normally associated with negative outcomes, success has a positive image. It is a conjunction of forces: right time, right place, right action, right use of will. A Chinese proverb says that success has an inherent balance. Like failure, though, success is a culmination, not a state of being. To be sustained, success requires you to steer a steady course in all conditions of weather and ocean, to navigate uncharted waters, and to visit unknown ports while maintaining clear focus on your destination.

Take credit for your success. You deserve personal recognition for achieving what you want.

Building a Sense of Self

As you will learn in greater detail later in this chapter, process is a series of events and experiences through which human transformation occurs.

On the following pages you will begin the first of several series of exercises that will help you chart successful goals. These exercises are process-oriented and self-directed. They have a single purpose: building a sense of self.

There are three components to building your sense of self. They include:

Experiencing self-sufficiency

Trusting yourself

Gaining a sense of direction

These components interact dynamically. Through observing your past behavior, thoughts, and feelings, reviewing your values, needs, and desires, and understanding your failures you will gain wisdom you can build on as you set your course for the future. The *Charting Your Goals* exercises are designed to facilitate this observing activity and help you develop your life-plan.

INSTRUCTIONS

In completing the following exercises, you may find these guidelines helpful:

Read the questions.

Listen to the answers that come to mind first.

Check the emotional response that accompanies that thought. Note that emotion briefly.

Ask yourself the question out loud.

Write down your answer.

This is a personal journal. We suggest that you write in the first person, use complete sentences, and be honest with yourself. **There are no right or wrong answers.**

When was the last time you failed at something important? Picture the incident clearly in your mind.

• What caused you to fail? What was your original intention?

_____

_____

_____

_____

_____

• What resulted from this failure that you did not like? How did you feel afterward?

_____

_____

_____

_____

_____

• Were you responsible for this failure, or did you blame someone else? Who did you blame? Why?

_____

_____

_____

_____

_____

• Do you more often tend to fail or succeed? _____

• What are the primary reasons you have for failing?

_____

_____

_____

_____

_____

_____

• As a child, how did you see your parents in terms of success and failure? Did they tend to fail or succeed at what they did?

_____

_____

_____

_____

• Were you ever punished for failing at something? Why?

_____

_____

_____

_____

• How are your attitudes about failure different from those of your parents?

_____

_____

_____

_____

_____

_____

_____

Relax, and let yourself feel comfortable. Recall your biggest success and picture the moment vividly in your mind.

Write a clear statement describing how it happened, what was behind it, and what made it the biggest.

_____

_____

_____

_____

_____

_____

_____

_____

_____

_____

_____

_____

_____

_____

_____

How did you feel at that time? Let yourself experience the same feeling now.

You are experiencing the feeling of success.

You should recall this feeling often as you go about your activities. **The more successful you feel, the more you open yourself to being successful.**

What will it take for you to feel like you have achieved success? Write a complete description of yourself as the most successful person you can envision. Describe yourself, your family and relationships, your health, your career and financial condition. What are you doing? How does it feel? Call this your **Picture of Success.**

_____

_____

_____

_____

_____

_____

_____

_____

_____

_____

_____

_____

_____

_____

_____

_____

_____

_____

_____

_____

_____

Power and Money

Goals and achieving success conjure visions of personal power and wealth. Power is the intentional use of influence over others' beliefs, behavior, and feelings. Wealth is having an abundance of material possessions and money.

Power must be used wisely if it is to be sustained. History provides countless examples of the misuse and loss of power. Military aggression, legislated poverty, and food as a political weapon are some generalized examples of the confusion between power and might. These examples illustrate the phrase "might is right"; that is, because one person or group has power over another, the stronger holds control. However, power that expresses itself as compelling force does not foster acceptance by those over whom the force is wielded and is usually lost in short order. In the context of life-planning, power may be sustained and enhanced by using it to further your personal growth and that of others in as many beneficial ways as possible.

As your success grows, you will begin to observe that power is structured, both formally and informally. The content and form of any power structure reflects the active level of conscious direction underlying it. For example, goals are power structures that succeed when you keep your energy and attention actively directed toward them.

The essence of goal achievement is accurate, adequate, and timely response to your present needs and perceived capabilities. As you clarify your personal values and identify your needs and wants, your goals will become increasingly attainable. The pattern of personal power that you have developed since childhood will become the springboard you use for success.

Your talents are clues to the most effective and efficient way for you to further develop your power and control your outcomes. The more you actively direct and take responsibility for your own talents and actions, the more you will be able to apply your resources to those activities which allow you to be more successful and, thereby, more powerful.

For you to respond accurately and adequately at the right time to any opportunity requires you to check your needs and wants frequently against your current inventory of resources and talents. Imagine that as you prepare for a voyage, you create lists of things you want to do and items you want to take along with you so that your trip is both successful and pleasurable. Since there is limited time before you leave and limited cargo space, you will want your lists to be prioritized and well-tailored to meet your actual needs. There is a natural balance between true assessment and fantasy. For example, if you are sailing across the north Atlantic in late winter, you must balance your need for warm clothing with any desires you have for exposing your body to the sun in the hope of arriving home with a "perfect" tan.

Your beliefs about who you are and what your capabilities and capacities are must be well founded. You should develop the practice of observing yourself so that you learn to appreciate your strengths as well as your weaknesses. This practice will help you begin to understand the limitations you have put upon yourself and the extent to which you are willing to grow or to change. Through this process you may find that you hold beliefs that either limit your ability or that of others to achieve success. If you believe that you are incapable of growing or changing, or assume that others are incapable of change, you may find that you are not able to achieve what you want. In holding this belief, you may also preclude others from helping you achieve your goals as well. Believing that you are limited by circumstances beyond your control will, in many cases, become an impediment to responding appropriately as changes arise. Outmoded beliefs give rise to fears that inhibit your ability to recognize opportunities that may work to your benefit.

Beliefs about power are manifested in many forms. Economic control, leadership in business and politics, decision responsibility, and ownership are examples of these manifestations. These forms may be used beneficially or destructively. You are ultimately responsible for how you use your own power.

How you use your personal power is closely associated with your will. Your desires, inclinations, appetites, passions, and choices influence and are influenced by how you use your personal power. You are in control of these factors at all times. **The key to using power successfully over time is being self-disciplined.**

Money comes from the advantageous use of resources. You have two primary resources for obtaining money: time and other money. Time is the most common resource expended for money. There may be a direct connection between your income and the amount of time you work. Money is the reward for your time. The next most common resource for producing money is other money. You may recall the adage that it takes money to make money. At its most essential level, this means investing for profit.

Acquiring money and managing it wisely will require you to use both time and money to your advantage. Advantage implies risk. Investment and risk go hand-in-hand. The level of profit is generally dependent upon the amount of risk associated with the investment. The higher the risk, the more the return will be, if the venture is successful. An example from the stock market illustrates this point. When you buy a stock it is likely that you have weighed its investment quality and assume that its value will rise. Nonetheless, you are probably buying it from someone equally convinced that its value is about to decline.

In the short term, it is generally much easier to redistribute current resources to improve your economic advantage than to acquire new ones. Inventorying these resources often results in uncovering hidden means already available for investment or deployment. Money management techniques have been the subject of many books, articles, and seminars. You should become familiar with what these formulas have to offer and adopt those which are tailored to your own financial objectives. As with power, economic self-discipline is a key to success.

If you operate from the viewpoint that the universe itself contains all of the elements it needs to support itself, you realize that whatever you need to accomplish your goals is either already present or available one way or another. This viewpoint also applies to money.

At times, you may perceive that your resources are insufficient to meet your needs. In that situation, do not panic and focus on the perceived scarcity but, instead, examine what alternatives may be available to you. Review your resources. It is the concept of plenty with which you should be most concerned.

YOUR VIEWPOINTS ABOUT POWER

There can be many objections to using power. Your experience has shaped your views. Use this opportunity to reflect on your viewpoints about power.

• Does your own power make you feel uncomfortable? How about the power of others? Remember a particular incident that you experienced. Describe your "level of comfort" at that time. How old were you when it happened?

_____

_____

_____

_____

_____

_____

_____

• Do you feel that you are a powerful person? Think back to an experience you had that gave you the feeling of being powerful. Describe what the experience was like for you.

_____

_____

_____

_____

_____

_____

_____

• Remember your picture of success. Look back at page 8. How much power does it take to be that successful? Describe what power you would need and how you would use that power to enhance and maintain your success.

_____

_____

_____

_____

_____

_____

_____

_____

_____

_____

_____

_____

_____

_____

_____

_____

_____

_____

_____

- Your viewpoints about money set the amount you now earn. How much money have you made over the last several years? Are you making as much as you need? Describe the optimal cash flow situation for you.

———————————————————————————————

———————————————————————————————

———————————————————————————————

———————————————————————————————

———————————————————————————————

———————————————————————————————

- How do you regularly spend your spare cash?

———————————————————————————————

———————————————————————————————

———————————————————————————————

———————————————————————————————

———————————————————————————————

———————————————————————————————

- Are you in debt? NO ——— YES ———

- Are all of your payments current? NO ——— YES ———

- Are there certain bills that you never seem to pay on time? NO ——— YES ———

- Describe what plan or plans you have for bringing your debts current and for paying them off.

———————————————————————————————

———————————————————————————————

———————————————————————————————

———————————————————————————————

———————————————————————————————

———————————————————————————————

• Remember the feeling and picture of your success. How much money does it take to be that successful? Describe how you would spend that money.

_____

_____

_____

_____

_____

_____

_____

_____

_____

_____

_____

_____

_____

_____

_____

_____

_____

_____

Time and Process

Success is not an accident. It has to do with being in the right place, at the right time, and taking the right action. The key factors that influence your ability to meet these requisites are time and process.

Time is a means of measuring periods between one event and another, or between an action and its consequence. In general, time is most often associated with the clock and calendar. Getting to work on time, celebrating holidays, meeting airline and train schedules, and looking forward to retirement are examples of how your life is ordered by hours, days, weeks, months, and years. In life-planning, time includes the period between now and the most distant future event you can imagine as well as whatever increments between those end points you determine are useful in the manifesting of your goals.

Process is your observation of and interchange with others or yourself. There are two types of process: individual and group. As an individual, you "process" your thoughts, feelings, and attitudes. You observe them internally in the constant dialogue that goes through your mind. As a member of a group, you may "process" common interests, attitudes, and observances. You will either agree or disagree with others, and they will either agree or disagree with you.

Time and process are frameworks for understanding your personal experience relative to others. How quickly you are able to reach your goals and the possible dependence of your success on that of someone else are examples of these frameworks. They illustrate a close cooperation between your pace and that of others and between your actions and those which others may take. Time and process assist you in allocating your resources, pacing your actions, and ordering your priorities. In this sense they facilitate your success.

Time and process are symbolic and mimic your viewpoints about them. This means that they are *relative* to your own experiences, rather than being set by some objective calculation or formula. You may find that your viewpoints about time and process often limit your experience and create boundaries that prevent you from being successful. Procrastination is a viewpoint about time with which you may be familiar. It is the belief that you are best served by putting off something you know you should do.

Similarly, sabotage is a viewpoint about process you may also recognize. It is the belief that you are best served by hampering or subverting the actions of yourself or others.

Time is a measure of dimension as well as a viewpoint. This measure may be friendly to your cause, or not. Establishing inflexible time frames may result in disappointing results and in feeling frustration when events do not meet your schedule.

Time is one of your most valuable resources. Its value lies in its perspective. This perspective allows you the flexibility you need to establish successful strategies and execute effective tactics. This flexibility is enhanced as you learn to befriend time.

The maxims of befriending time are:

- **Always expect the unexpected.**

    No matter how you prepare, expect something to occur that you have not expected. Contract and expand your scale of measurement and adjust your expectations to changing circumstances. Your critical milestones are often independent of time measures.

    Do not confuse your time lines for achieving success with those of inter-mediating or unexpected events that seem to delay your progress. Imagine that your voyage includes a number of ports of call before you reach your destination. You may have set a time table for reaching each port. If, however, you happen to like a particular place very much, you may decide to spend more time there than you had originally planned. Or, if your boat needs unanticipated repairs, similar changes of schedule may occur. All things being equal, reaching each port is the set of critical milestones; whether you stay at each a day, a week, or a month, is entirely up to you!

- **Pause.**

    Give yourself breathing space when you are confronted by barriers. Obstacles often arise without warning. They may be the result of the crosscurrent of another's progress or the intervention of something not in your control. A powerful action in such a situation is to pause, which means to stop action for the moment.

Timing is an important factor when you deliberately stop an action. If you wait too long to resume action or change course, procrastination may overtake you and set the stage for failure. Pausing presumes your continuing awareness of the internal or external cause that necessitates this delaying tactic.

———————————— BEFRIENDING PROCESS ————————————

Your ability to befriend time will enhance those abilities needed for you to use process effectively for your benefit. Remember, in life-planning, process refers to your observation of and interchange with others or yourself. Using process effectively requires an understanding of the dynamics of personal and human interchange.

The cornerstone of effective personal and interpersonal interchange is self-discipline. Self-discipline means regulating your own actions for the sake of self-improvement and achievement. The practice of self-discipline allows you to be discerning and discriminating in your actions. Self-discipline, in turn, is sustained by self-knowledge. In other words, you must observe and come to know yourself intimately.

Many theoretical and practical models have been developed to facilitate self-knowledge. Reflection, meditation, psychotherapy, and sports are examples of these models. Some work better than others. Choose those which work for you. Be practical. Learn the techniques of your model and practice them. Become skilled. Consider it an art form or a lifestyle.

Whatever your practice, be kind to yourself and others.

It is important to maintain balance in your process with others and yourself. The more balance you maintain the easier it is for you to direct your actions and influence those of others.

Remember these simple rules:

- Know thyself.
- Consider others.

Your achievements are not accomplished in a vacuum. Often, they are socially dependent. The resources that you may need to accomplish a goal may need to be shared with others. A part of sharing involves managing your time so that potential conflicts are minimized.

Give your time and attention to others generously. You will be repaid with enthusiasm and support for your goals that cannot be gained in any other way. When you set your time frames consider both their dependencies and effects upon others.

Your desire for success is potentially as great as that of any other person. Any number of sailors may want to reach the same destination as you. If you fail to follow the established rules of the waterway your ship may collide with another. **Be kind.**

• How did you learn to tell time? Who taught you and how old were you?

_____

_____

_____

• Remember the last time you were late. What was the occasion? Do you remember how people reacted? Are you late frequently?

_____

_____

_____

_____

• Are there many occasions when you do not have enough time to get things done? Why?

_____

_____

_____

_____

• Are the days getting shorter and the years going by faster? Why?

_____

_____

_____

• Do you remember the place you played most often as a child? Have you returned to that place as an adult? How did it seem different?

_____

_____

_____

_____

Be comfortable. Sit back and relax.

Take a deep breath and exhale slowly.

Remember your feeling and picture of success. Review page 8. Re-create that feeling now.

- Who are you in this situation?
- How do you feel about yourself?
- Are you happy?
- Do you expect to change your life for the better?
- How much change is comfortable for you?
- Are you motivated and self-disciplined?

Answer each of the questions to your own satisfaction. If you answer "No" to any of the questions, you should examine your reasons.

Remember the adage of Greece, "Know thyself." Each of us has areas of growth. It is important for you to know what yours are and how you may need to grow. Use self-observation as a means of knowing how successful you are and of building self-discipline.

two

YOUR RESOURCES

In this chapter, you will look closely at:

- Your resources
- Your values
- Your images

You will have the opportunity to see how your viewpoints have established boundaries—or limits—that are useful to you as you describe your own personal reality. Your description of reality may vary from that of your neighbor, in whole or in part.

Your resources include time, energy, money, and other "raw materials" you have available for your use. These resources dictate, in great measure, what you are able to spend in the pursuit of success. Similarly, your values are strong operatives and reflect the beliefs you have about one thing or another. How your values, in turn, influence the deployment of your resources is explained through the images and metaphors you use to describe your reality. Images and metaphors provide powerful tools that will facilitate your life-planning process.

An understanding of your resources, values, and images will provide you with information which you may quantify and examine. That understanding will assist you in achieving your goals.

Inventories

Desires are signals about your goals. They indicate potential directions and actions. In this context, desire is a resource. You have other resources as well. Some are immediately available for use, others are not. The purpose of this section is to inventory your resources.

The following pages provide you with space to inventory your resources in five basic categories:

- Health
- Relationships
- Personal Growth
- Finances
- Career

You may find that there are other categories of resources that are important to you in addition to these five. We recommend, however, that you start with these.

In general, the topics you will cover within these categories are self-evident. Health, relationships, finances, and career are commonly used terms. Personal growth, however, may need further explanation. Personal growth refers to those aspirations or ambitions you may have for developing your individual talents. For example, personal growth topics include education, spiritual pursuits, hobbies, self-improvement, and other interests not related to the other categories.

The best way to approach this inventory exercise is to brainstorm. Do not spend too much time looking for the "right answer" to each question.

Follow your first thoughts; skip from one category to another if you wish. If you find you cannot get past a certain point, leave it and go to something else.

Each inventory includes questions to help you focus your attention on your current state of health, the quality of your relationships, how you hope to grow, your financial condition, and your career aspirations.
The key questions are:

- **What are your current themes?**
  Briefly list your recurring thoughts about this topic. For example, better health, more money, closer relations, etc. Be as complete as possible. These are your agendas.

- **What do you want?**
  "If I could have anything at all . . ." Describe the things you want. What would you like to have? Buy? Get? Make? Learn? Give? Enjoy? Do?

- **What obstacles have you experienced in the past?**
  What's always standing in the way? What are the roadblocks you may face in the future?

- **What failures have you had?**
  Write down all the significant failures you may have experienced.

- **What are your hopes for the future? Your fears?**
  Hopes and fears about a goal tend to go hand-in-hand. What do you hope for and fear most about achieving your goals in this category?

- **How do you picture the ideal future?**
  Imagine that you can have what you want. What picture does that create?

- **How close is your future?**
  How long do you think it will take for you to achieve the picture you have just imagined? Will it happen today? Tomorrow? Next week? Next month? Next year? Be as accurate as you can.

Do you have any health concerns? NO _____ YES _____

In terms of maintaining or changing your current state of health:

• What are your current themes?

_____

_____

_____

_____

• What do you want?

_____

_____

_____

_____

_____

_____

_____

_____

_____

_____

_____

• What obstacles have you experienced in the past?

_____

_____

_____

_____

- What failures have you had?

_____

_____

_____

- What are your hopes for the future? Your fears?

_____

_____

_____

_____

_____

- How do you picture the ideal future?

_____

_____

_____

_____

_____

_____

_____

_____

_____

- How close is your future?

_____

_____

_____

_____

YOUR RESOURCES: RELATIONSHIPS INVENTORY

Do you have any concerns about your relationships? NO ____ YES ____

In terms of maintaining or changing your current relationships:

• What are your current themes?

_____

_____

_____

_____

_____

• What do you want?

_____

_____

_____

_____

_____

_____

_____

_____

_____

_____

_____

• What obstacles have you experienced in the past?

_____

_____

_____

- What failures have you had?

  _____

  _____

  _____

- What are your hopes for the future? Your fears?

  _____

  _____

  _____

  _____

  _____

- How do you picture the ideal future?

  _____

  _____

  _____

  _____

  _____

  _____

  _____

  _____

  _____

- How close is your future?

  _____

  _____

  _____

  _____

YOUR RESOURCES: PERSONAL GROWTH INVENTORY

Do you have any concerns about your personal growth? NO ___ YES ___

In terms of maintaining or changing your personal growth:

• What are your current themes?

_____

_____

_____

• What do you want?

_____

_____

_____

_____

_____

_____

_____

_____

_____

_____

_____

• What obstacles have you experienced in the past?

_____

_____

_____

_____

_____

• What failures have you had?

_____

_____

_____

• What are your hopes for the future? Your fears?

_____

_____

_____

_____

_____

• How do you picture the ideal future?

_____

_____

_____

_____

_____

_____

_____

_____

_____

• How close is your future?

_____

_____

_____

_____

YOUR RESOURCES: FINANCIAL INVENTORY

Do you have any concerns about your financial condition? NO ___ YES ___

In terms of maintaining or changing your financial condition:

• What are your current themes?

_____

_____

_____

• What do you want?

_____

_____

_____

_____

_____

_____

_____

_____

_____

_____

• What obstacles have you experienced in the past?

_____

_____

_____

_____

_____

• What failures have you had?

_____

_____

_____

• What are your hopes for the future? Your fears?

_____

_____

_____

_____

_____

• How do you picture the ideal future?

_____

_____

_____

_____

_____

_____

_____

_____

_____

_____

• How close is your future?

_____

_____

_____

_____

Do you have any concerns about your career? NO _____ YES _____

In terms of maintaining or changing your present career:

• What are your current themes?

_____

_____

_____

• What do you want?

_____

_____

_____

_____

_____

_____

_____

_____

_____

_____

• What obstacles have you experienced in the past?

_____

_____

_____

_____

_____

- What failures have you had?

_____

_____

_____

- What are your hopes for the future? Your fears?

_____

_____

_____

_____

_____

- How do you picture the ideal future?

_____

_____

_____

_____

_____

_____

_____

_____

_____

- How close is your future?

_____

_____

_____

_____

Values

Values are standards or qualities which you consider worthwhile or desirable. Values help you to establish your sense of purpose and direction, and act as guideposts that assist you in measuring the quality of your life.

Every day you are confronted by a myriad of choices, most of which require almost no thought. You respond to them intuitively. Others, however, require careful consideration, a weighing of options, or quiet reflection. You respond to these intellectually. Your personal values influence both your intuitive and intellectual decision-making. Often the choice you make is highly influenced by one or more of the values you hold. For example, the career you decide to have, the kind of relationships you attract, and the way you choose to live reflect your values about career, relationships, and life.

The importance of understanding your values lies in the insight you gain about your decision-making processes. Your personal satisfaction is highly dependent upon the quality of your decisions. If you make decisions which are consistent with your values, you will experience a sense of comfort that you made the right choice. If, however, your decisions are not aligned with your values, you will probably experience a sense of discomfort and concern. For example, if you have good health as an important value and you decide to smoke cigarettes you may find yourself trying to rationalize your decision. Such actions set up internal contradictions. What is more important: good health or smoking cigarettes? Until you resolve the contradiction, you will experience the tension or stress which the contradiction creates in you. You can generally tell whether your decisions are consistent with your values by how happy you are. Your decisions affect you, as well as your health, your relationships, your personal growth, your finances, and your career.

All people seek satisfaction; that is, they aspire to experience the fulfillment of their desires and needs. Your pursuit of satisfaction is your desire to be fulfilled and gratified. It is a natural phenomenon. Each level of attainment becomes the baseline for experiencing future achievements. As you experience one level of fulfillment, your appetite grows and you pursue greater satisfaction. Seeking to be satisfied is representative and symptomatic of Nature's Way of helping you grow and ensuring that you care for yourself. The human process of acquiring experiences that fulfill the desire for satisfaction emanates from the need for survival, the necessity of human communication, and the pursuit of meaning in your life.

Take a minute to think about your own values. Clear your mind and relax. Ask yourself:

- What's really important to you?
- Have you ever been in a situation where you had to support or defend something that was not important to you?
- When was the last time you really felt satisifed? What was the emotion you experienced? Feel that emotion now. The emotion you are feeling is that of satisfaction.

Clarifying Your Values

On the next page, you will find a list of values. Not all of those which are listed may be important to you. Some people have values that are different from yours. Also, you may have values that you have not thought about before.

The purpose of the exercises in this section is for you to clarify your values. You will have the opportunity to reflect upon your values concerning each of the five categories in which you have already reviewed your resources, and to choose those which are important to you for closer examination.

These exercises are thought-provoking and may take time. Do not hurry. Read through the list and think about what each value means to you. You may want to add any values of your own that are not included; you may want to eliminate others. Then, go through the list again and highlight those which you consider to be influential in your life.

Accomplishment
Achievement
Activity
Admiration
Advancement
Advantage
Adventure
Advocacy
Affection
Affluence
Age
Ambition
America
Appearance
Art Appreciation
Artistic Expression
Athletics
Authenticity
Authority
Autonomy

Beauty
Belonging
Brotherhood
Business

Career
Caring
Challenge
Charity
Clarity
Close Friends
Club Membership
College Degree
Comfort
Commitments
Competition
Conformity
Connections
Conservation
Consistency
Control
Cooperation
Country
Country Focus
Country Living
Crafts
Creativity
Credit
Culture

Decisiveness
Dining Out
Discipline
Docility
Dominance
Drama
Duty

Eating
Economic Security
Education
Employment

Endurance
Energy
Enjoyment
Enterprise
Entertainment
Entrepreneurship
Environment
Equality
Equal Opportunity
Eternal Life
Exciting Life
Exercise
Experience
Experimentation

Faith
Fame
Family
Family Orientation
Family Security
Flamboyance
Free Choice
Freedom
Free Time
Friendship
Frivolity
Fun

God's Will
Golden Rule
Good Income
Goodness
Gracious Living
Guiding

Happiness
Healing
Health
Health Insurance
Helping Others
High Standards
Holiness
Home
Honesty
Honor
Hope
Humility
Humor

Imagination
Improving Society
Impulse
Income
Independence
Individualism
Industriousness
Influence over Others
Inner Direction
Inner Guide
Inner Harmony
Innovation
Insurance
Integrity

Intellectual Stimulation
Interpersonal Relations
Intimacy
Involvement

Joviality
Joy

Lack of Pretense
Laughter
Leadership
Leisure
Life
Life Insurance
Literature
Love
Lover
Loyalty

Managing
Mastery
Materialism
Maturity
Meditation
Mentoring
Metaphysics
Military
Millions
Modesty
Money
Morality

National Security
Neatness
New Car
Nonconformity
Nurturance

Obedience
Order
Outdoor Life
Ownership

Participating with Others
Patience
Peace
Peacefulness
Persistence
Personal Development
Philanthropy
Philosophy
Play
Pleasure
Politics
Possessions
Power
Process
Production
Professionalism
Prosperity
Psychic Power

Reading
Rebellion

Recognition
Religion
Religious Beliefs
Reputation
Respect
Respectfulness
Responsibility
Retirement
Rewards
Riches

Satisfaction
Schedule
Security
Self-Expression
Self-Reliance
Self-Respect
Self-Satisfaction
Servants
Sincerity
Social Life
Social Power
Social Recognition
Social Relations
Space
Spirituality
Sports
Stability
Stamina
Standing up for Beliefs
Status
Stimulation
Suburban Focus
Suburban Living
Success
Survival

Taking Risks
Teamwork
Technique
Tenacity
Tradition
Tranquility
Travel
Trust
Truth
Truthfulness

Urban Focus
Urban Living

Wealth
Welfare
Well-Being
Who's Who
Winning
Wisdom
Work

Youth

Zeal
Zest

Value Priorities

Your values influence your decisions about your relationships, your personal growth, your finances, and your career. For example, your health may be influenced by values of athletics, beauty, eating, exercise, self-mastery, and survival. Your personal growth may, in turn, be influenced by your health. Write down the values that influence you most in each of the following areas:

HEALTH

_____

_____

_____

_____

_____

_____

_____

RELATIONSHIPS

_____

_____

_____

_____

_____

_____

_____

_____

PERSONAL GROWTH

_____

_____

_____

_____

_____

_____

FINANCES

_____

_____

_____

_____

_____

_____

CAREER

_____

_____

_____

_____

_____

_____

Consider what each of the values you have chosen means for you. For example, if you hold "stamina" as a health-related value, think about how you would describe, quantify, or illustrate the meaning that "stamina" has for you. What are the things you are doing in your present health practices to maintain or increase your stamina? What else about stamina is important for you?

You may find that some values are more important for you than others. For example, economic security may be a more important value in your financial plan than credit or competition.

On the following pages, prioritize the values you have for each category and define what each value means for you. Your definitions should be as precise as possible. If you say that "challenge" is your most important personal growth value, for example, what are the types of challenges to which you are referring? Is there a particular challenge that comes to mind? Or, if "equal opportunity" is your most important career value, what are the situations you are facing where equal opportunity is an issue?

The goal of this exercise is for you to understand how your values influence your decisions about your health, relationships, personal growth, financial condition, and career.

Prioritize your health values and describe what each one means for you.

1 _____

_____

2 _____

_____

3 _____

_____

4 _____

_____

5 _____

_____

6 _____

_____

7 _____

_____

8 _____

_____

9 _____

_____

10 _____

_____

Prioritize your relationship values and describe what each one means for you.

1 _____

_____

2 _____

_____

3 _____

_____

4 _____

_____

5 _____

_____

6 _____

_____

7 _____

_____

8 _____

_____

9 _____

_____

10 _____

_____

YOUR RESOURCES: PERSONAL GROWTH VALUES

Prioritize your personal growth values and describe what each one means for you.

1 _____

_____

2 _____

_____

3 _____

_____

4 _____

_____

5 _____

_____

6 _____

_____

7 _____

_____

8 _____

_____

9 _____

_____

10 _____

_____

YOUR RESOURCES: FINANCIAL VALUES

Prioritize your financial values and describe what each one means for you.

1 _____

_____

2 _____

_____

3 _____

_____

4 _____

_____

5 _____

_____

6 _____

_____

7 _____

_____

8 _____

_____

9 _____

_____

10 _____

_____

Prioritize your career values and describe what each one means for you.

1 _____

_____

2 _____

_____

3 _____

_____

4 _____

_____

5 _____

_____

6 _____

_____

7 _____

_____

8 _____

_____

9 _____

_____

10 _____

_____

Values point to your current needs and agendas for internal change.

Clarity of purpose and direction comes from an organized personal plan. The value clarification that you have just completed is the springboard for the *Charting Your Goals* process, which you will begin in the next chapter. The unique blend of your personal values and the relative priority of your needs and wants establish the foundation for your life-plan.

The images and the metaphors you use to describe your life-plan are the tools you use to link your values to the world of action and achievement. Before you begin charting your goals, you need to investigate how the imaging process works. The following section provides that opportunity.

Images and Metaphors

Images are visual pictures or sensory likenesses of yourself, and of persons, places, things, and situations. When you "picture something in your mind" or recall the feelings of a particularly wonderful time you are creating images.

Metaphors are descriptions of your experiences. They are stories which relate your personal experiences to general observations about life and allow you to share your experiences with others. How you elaborate on an adventure from your past for the benefit of a friend, the context in which you justify certain actions you may have taken, and the description you give of something that is important to you are examples of metaphors.

What makes these mental pictures and verbal descriptions so important in a life-planning context is that they give you insight about your own self-image and provide an excellent means of better understanding how you formed that image of yourself.

Your self-image affects how you achieve your goals and is, in turn, affected by your successes and failures. If, for example, you have an image of yourself that is beautiful, you will be attractive and you will tend to describe yourself to others in terms that portray you that way. If, however, your self-image is that you are overweight or ill-proportioned, you may not feel attractive and it may be hard for you to present yourself credibly as a handsome person. In some ways, your images of yourself and your circumstances as well as the metaphors you have created to describe those images act as self-fulfilling prophecies. In relaying your images to others, the metaphors you use to describe yourself will tell you more about your self-image.

It is very hard to achieve something that you cannot visualize or describe in a way which is believable to you. It is your own beliefs which are important, not those of others who may have judgments about who you are, what you have, or what you have been able to accomplish. However, you cannot expect others to believe that you can be who you want to be and have what you want to have if you do not believe it yourself!

Imagine that you are introducing yourself to someone special. Imagine that this person is also the key to your success in achieving a critical goal. On the following pages, write a description of yourself, as if you were telling it to this person. Present your best image. You should include information about the following areas:

- Who you are and where you are from
- Your most important achievements
- What you think of yourself
- What you intend to accomplish during the next 90 days and how you intend to accomplish it
- Any personal information you feel you want to share with this person

Think of this exercise as one wherein you convey to this person who you really are and what you really want. Say what your true aspirations are. Go back to the **picture of success** you described in chapter 1 (on page 8) for ideas.

Be as lengthy or concise as you feel is necessary to tell your story.

Ultimately, your private reflection about the images and metaphors you use in descriptions such as these leads to a better understanding of your self-image.

You cannot achieve goals that are inconsistent with your self-image.

For example, if your self-image is one wherein you picture yourself as fat, it is likely that you are and will remain overweight until you change your self-image. Similarly, if your self-image is that you are well proportioned for your size, strong and healthy, your body is more apt to take on the form of one who manifests those qualities. You will find that your self-image motivates you to take appropriate steps to achieve your goals.

If you have a goal which is inconsistent with your self-image, you have two options:

- You may change your goal.
- You may change your self-image.

Since your viewpoints shape the images that tend to limit or enhance your experiences, ensuring consistency between your goals and self-image is an exercise that supports achieving your ideal needs and wants. **If you want to look a particular way, attract a particular type of partner, or have a satisfying career, you need to develop and visualize yourself looking like, attracting, and having what you want.**

As you begin *Charting Your Goals,* you should practice image-making and develop metaphors that describe you as the achiever of your goals. Think about and describe to yourself all aspects of your life and behavior as if your goals are already a reality.

three
CHARTING YOUR GOALS

In this chapter, you will have the opportunity to explore the dynamics of goal achievement and create your life-plan. You will examine:

- Goal dynamics, or how planning and achievement processes work.
- Needs, wants, and images, which are the foundations on which you set realistic and achievable goals.
- Goals, strategies, and tactics, which are your objectives and the course you will chart to attain them.

Your objective, in this chapter, is to chart your goals. This process involves:

- Identifying your needs and wants.
- Imaging your course.
- Setting your goals.
- Developing the strategies and tactics necessary for success.

You will set your goals to satisfy your needs and wants, aim your strategies to optimize your chances of success, and then execute your tactics to achieve your goals.

50

Planning and Goal Dynamics

There are three things which are necessary to achieve a goal:

1. **Place your attention on the goal.**
   Be aware of what you really want. Create a clear mental picture of your goals. If you want to have a career that's more satisfying, begin to paint a mental picture of everything about that career that you want. If it's to take a vacation, begin to take mental photographs of your ideal vacation spot.

2. **Intend that you will achieve it.**
   Place your mind on the process of achieving. For example, think positive thoughts and make positive statements about reaching your goals.

3. **Be willing to receive whatever comes.**
   Dispose yourself to receive what you want. Look carefully at how you have imagined your goals. What you actually achieve is the natural outcome of your commitment to reach that goal.

This dynamic is the core of the *Charting Your Goals* life-planning method. Imagine this dynamic at work as you set sail for some distant shore. You decide where you want to go (place your attention on your destination), make the necessary preparations (focus your intention on the things necessary to make your trip a success), and set sail (be receptive, or trust that you will reach your destination).

Once you have set your goals you need a plan for achieving them. A plan is a detailed scheme, program, or method worked out beforehand for the accomplishment of an objective.

Many methods of planning work, some better than others. Different types of planning are appropriate for different tasks. For example, the plans for a cruise include all aspects of the preparations and maneuvers necessary for the ship to sail as well as those needed to ensure a safe and enjoyable voyage for the passengers. Similarly, many businesses have complex systems to monitor their performance and profitability objectives. A short trip to the grocery store, however, requires much simpler arrangements.

Charting Your Goals uses a specially designed chart and planning process to help you set your goals and develop the strategies and tactics necessary to achieve them.

Most successful plans contain three major elements:

- A clear objective.
- A time frame and method within which the objective is to be achieved.
- A delineation of the steps necessary to achieve the objective.

Good plans are based on a careful analysis of the facts which may be relevant both to the objective and to any of the steps needed to accomplish it. Therefore, in establishing a plan, examine all of the relevant facts, consider all of the possible outcomes, and weigh contingencies carefully. One way of doing that is for you to consider what the best and the worst possible developments may be. For example, if you want to change jobs, consider what the most optimistic career opportunity may be as well as that which is least desirable. What are the consequences of each? If the best materializes, your income, professional status, and job satisfaction increase. In the worst case, your job opportunity may not materialize. If you quit your current position and are confronted with the worst case scenario, you may find yourself unemployed. Take each step further. What changes will a new job bring to your primary relationships, your health, and the amount of time you have for recreation? Can you afford to be unemployed? This is a short example of the direct, no-nonsense questions you need to ask in setting up your life-plan.

In order to plan successfully, it is important to observe what works for you. Some of you will feel very comfortable with a method of planning that is highly organized and well documented. Others of you are more comfortable with a planning formula that makes minimal demands on your time. Wherever in this spectrum you are, develop and use a method that works well for you.

For this exercise, focus on a particular planning experience that may have worked well for you in the past. It may have been a plan for finding a job, or one for a wedding or some other occasion where you were responsible for its success.

• Remember the plan and describe its important aspects.

_____

_____

_____

_____

_____

• What was it about your plan that made it successful? Consider what might have happened if you had used another plan.

_____

_____

_____

_____

_____

• How much planning do you do now for the future?

_____

_____

• Do you ever overplan?

_____

_____

• Do you feel that you have planned sufficiently for your future? If not, what else do you think is necessary?

_____

_____

_____

Goal achievement is a nonlinear process that occurs in multidimensions of time, place, and circumstance. Often you may get exactly what you want; other times what you get may not be exactly what you asked for; sometimes you may feel disappointed.

The goal achievement dynamic is based on the principles of

- Attention
- Intention
- Receptivity

The **principle of attention** describes the process of focusing the mind on an object of sensation or of thought, which results in the production of a clear image of your goal. Ongoing attention—that is, keeping focused over time—requires you to develop your ability to concentrate on what you want and to integrate maximally your higher mental processes. In the *Charting Your Goals* process, the principle of attention is described as the focusing of awareness on a particular goal.

The **principle of intention** underlies your determination to act in a certain way. Your intention is how you convey your feelings of purpose about reaching your objectives. Your intention is either clear-cut—you know what your goal is and that you will reach it—or you may be undecided about achieving your goals to win.

The **principle of receptivity** establishes your willingness to have what you want. Wanting a strong and healthy body and having one are distinctly different actions. In the same vein, knowing that you always get what you need allows you to grow in your ability to have more. *Charting Your Goals* views this principle as your consent to have what you want and accept what comes to you.

When these principles operate together, achievement results.

You will see how that works in your own life-plan. As you set your goals, your attention is directed to the images you have created about your goals. As your attention becomes more focused, you will face decisions about what you need to do to reach your goals. By creating positive images and holding the intention that you will succeed, you become more receptive to the actualizing of your goals.

It is a simple process, but one that requires careful consideration. Take the time to reflect on your dreams, your needs, and your wants and think through what it takes to make those dreams come true.

Charting Your Goals uses a chart to map all of the elements necessary to manage goal achievement dynamics effectively. Each chart is divided into eight sections:

CHARTING YOUR GOALS

Values		Commitments	
Needs	Images	Goals	Strategies
Wants			Tactics

On the left side of each chart, there are areas for you to list and describe your values, your needs, your wants, and your images about the topic of each chart. On the right, there are areas for you to set and plan your goals, strategies, and tactics, and to describe the commitments you are willing to make to ensure your own success.

Individual charts have been provided for you to chart your goals for health, relationships, personal growth, finances, and career. The charts you will use as you continue *Charting Your Goals* are located at the end of this chapter. You should refer to them and use them as a means of collecting and organizing your thoughts as you complete the remaining exercises. On the following pages are two examples of how to use the charts.

CHARTING YOUR GOALS

Values

Entrepreneurship
Prosperity

Needs

I need more fulfilling work.

I need to be independent.

I need to direct my own work.

I need more freedom of choice.

I need to get out of corporate life.

I need a more flexible schedule.

I need to do what I like to do and make a lot of profit.

Wants

I want to make more money.

I want more artistic expression in my work.

I want more project-oriented work.

I want less structure and organizational rules.

I want less bureaucracy at work.

I want to work with more passion.

Images

I see myself in a flexible, more creative workday.

I see myself more joyful about doing my work.

I see myself being largely successful.

I see others acknowledging my newfound success.

I hear publicity over the radio and television about my new business.

I hear joyful praise coming from my mother and family.

I feel happy about my decision to be an independent entrepreneur.

I feel physically/emotionally fulfilled by my new work.

I feel my clients are completely satisfied.

I feel rich.

Commitments

I commit myself to the creation of the most successful business venture of my life, which will assist millions of people and win fame, riches, and be an original, creative expression.

Goals

I want to create a new business which directs my clients to career and other life fulfillment.

I want to make $300,000 in the first year of operation.

I want to be a successful media figure.

Strategies

I will appear as much in the media as possible in the next 90 days.

I will resign my current position by October 1st.

I will complete my current book project.

I will rearrange my finances to accommodate my new goal.

I will deliver seminars.

Tactics

Compile radio and TV target broadcast list by 9/15.

Successfully terminate my current corporate position by 10/1.

Self-publish my book by 9/1 and write a book proposal by 9/7.

Schedule fall seminars by 9/1.

Draft brochure copy by 9/1.

Create an office at home by 8/25.

Write a newspaper article by 10/1.

CHARTING YOUR GOALS

Values

Energy	Appearance	Nurturance
Stamina	Endurance	Pleasure
Beauty	Healing	Satisfaction

Needs

I need strength and stamina to face and overcome my current health challenges.

I need flexibility.

I need to follow a good exercise program.

I need to have a nutritionally sound diet.

Wants

I want a muscular, youthful body.

I want to be able to engage in healthy physical activities, especially:

• Swimming
• Racquetball
• Sailing

I want to mitigate the negative effects of stress on my body by maintaining a health regimen.

I want to remain relaxed and alert.

Images

I experience healing of those physical challenges that I now face, including:

• Repairing the bone in my left foot
• Achieving the weight I want
• Developing my sense of smell
• Controlling my addiction to sugar

I visualize myself looking my best and experience that I have:

• 30″ waist
• 14% body fat
• 42″ chest
• 15″ biceps

I am experiencing maximum physical strength, endurance, and vitality.

I am relaxed and able to respond appropriately to physical challenges and stress.

Commitments

I am committed to doing what needs to be done so that I have perfect health and reach all of my goals.

Goals

I want good health, a long life, and a happy death. Long life means living at least 100 years with full physical capacity and mental clarity.

I want to achieve and maintain optimal physical condition, including:

- Abundant energy and agility (physical and mental alertness and briskness)
- Above average aerobic stamina and strength (physical power)
- Excellent muscular development
- A high degree of flexibility
- Focused mental processes and clear thinking
- Clear eyes and skin and attractive appearance
- The finest sensory abilities and an open speaking voice

Strategies

Maintain my daily health regimen concerning diet, exercise, and relaxation, including:

- Weight train three times each week.
- 60 minutes of aerobic exercise at least five times each week.
- Follow my diet.
- Meditate for at least 30 minutes each day.
- Participate in sports that feel good.
- Get at least seven hours' sleep each night.

I will keep a clear head and remember everything.

I will maintain an average weight of 160 pounds.

I will engage my mind totally with body during every exercise session.

I will think positive thoughts and maintain positive images about my health.

Tactics

Go to the gym.

Meditate.

Set up a racquetball game.

Weigh myself.

No desserts today!

Practice positive thinking.

Needs and Wants

It is important to distinguish between your needs and your wants.

Your needs include anything which you perceive to be necessary for your personal well-being. For example, most people have needs for adequate shelter, clothing, food; many people also need cars, love, acceptance, beauty; others need career, flexibility, physical fitness, self-confidence.

Your needs may be many and varied, or they may be few and consistent. Whatever they are, you should consider them your highest priority. Having your essential needs taken care of allows you to feel secure. That feeling is the basis for believing that you are safe and sound. Experiencing this feeling is fundamental to the pursuit of happiness.

Your wants are anything for which you have a strong desire but that may not be essential for your personal well-being. For example, you may need a better job and determine that you want a new outfit to impress a prospective interviewer. Or, you may need to improve your level of physical fitness and want to join a gym. Sometimes you may need food and want a piece of chocolate cake.

There is a common perception that needs often require a longer time frame for fulfillment than do wants. Although, in general, your wants are not of higher priority than your needs, a particular want may be your most pressing priority. That occurs when immediate gratification is important.

In the following exercises, you will have the opportunity to identify your needs and wants in each of the five *Charting Your Goals* categories.

IDENTIFYING YOUR HEALTH NEEDS AND WANTS

• What do you need to feel healthy? Be specific and list everything you believe you need.

_____

_____

_____

_____

_____

_____

_____

• Assuming your health needs are met, what else do you want that relates to your health? Be specific and list everything you want.

_____

_____

_____

_____

_____

_____

_____

• Are there any obstacles that are keeping you from meeting and satisfying your health needs or wants? If so, what are they?

_____

_____

_____

_____

_____

- What do you need to feel that your relationships are satisfying? Be specific and list everything you believe you need.

_____

_____

_____

_____

_____

_____

_____

- Assuming your relationship needs are met, what else do you want that relates to them? Be specific and list everything you want.

_____

_____

_____

_____

_____

_____

_____

- Are there any obstacles that are keeping you from meeting and satisfying your relationship needs or wants? If so, what are they?

_____

_____

_____

_____

_____

- What do you need to feel that you are growing and satisfied? Be specific and list everything you believe you need.

_____

_____

_____

_____

_____

_____

_____

- Assuming your personal growth needs are met, what else do you want that relates to them? Be specific and list everything you want.

_____

_____

_____

_____

_____

_____

_____

- Are there any obstacles that are keeping you from meeting and satisfying your personal growth needs or wants? If so, what are they?

_____

_____

_____

_____

_____

- What do you need to feel satisfied about your finances? Be specific and list everything you believe you need.

_____

_____

_____

_____

_____

_____

_____

- Assuming your financial needs are met, what else do you want that relates to them? Be specific and list everything you want.

_____

_____

_____

_____

_____

_____

_____

- Are there any obstacles that are keeping you from meeting and satisfying your financial needs or wants? If so, what are they?

_____

_____

_____

_____

IDENTIFYING YOUR CAREER NEEDS AND WANTS

• What do you need to feel satisfied about your career? Be specific and list everything you believe you need.

_____

_____

_____

_____

_____

_____

_____

• Assuming your career needs are met, what else do you want that relates to them? Be specific and list everything you want.

_____

_____

_____

_____

_____

_____

_____

• Are there any obstacles that are keeping you from meeting and satisfying your career needs or wants? If so, what are they?

_____

_____

_____

_____

_____

Creating Images

Once you have identified your needs and wants, it is important for you to imagine having them satisfied. Visualize this occurring. What does it feel like? Describe this feeling. Begin to develop pictures of yourself and the circumstances surrounding the gratification of your needs and wants. Create that picture using the imaging techniques you began to practice in the previous chapter.

To be effective, images must be tangible. Your descriptions should include:

- What you see and hear
- How you feel
- What you are doing

In the following exercises you will have the opportunity to build images of yourself meeting and satisfying the needs and wants you have already identified.

• Imagine yourself satisfying all of your health needs. How do you feel?

_____

_____

_____

_____

_____

_____

_____

_____

_____

_____

• Describe how you see yourself when you have the health you want. Be as precise as possible.

_____

_____

_____

_____

_____

_____

_____

_____

_____

_____

• Do you have any feelings or pictures about your health that you want to change? If so, what are they?

_____

_____

_____

_____

_____

_____

_____

_____

_____

• Assume you have changed these feelings or pictures. Describe how you feel and what pictures you have as a result of the change.

_____

_____

_____

_____

_____

_____

_____

_____

_____

• Imagine yourself satisfying all of your relationship needs. How do you feel?

_____

_____

_____

_____

_____

_____

_____

_____

_____

_____

• Describe how you see yourself when you have the relationships you want. Be as precise as possible.

_____

_____

_____

_____

_____

_____

_____

_____

_____

_____

• Do you have any feelings or pictures about your relationships that you want to change? If so, what are they?

_____

_____

_____

_____

_____

_____

_____

_____

_____

_____

• Assume you have changed these feelings or pictures. Describe how you feel and what pictures you have as a result of the change.

_____

_____

_____

_____

_____

_____

_____

_____

_____

_____

CREATING IMAGES ABOUT YOUR PERSONAL GROWTH

• Imagine yourself satisfying all of your personal growth needs. How do you feel?

_____

_____

_____

_____

_____

_____

_____

_____

_____

• Describe how you see yourself when you have the personal growth opportunities you want. Be as precise as possible.

_____

_____

_____

_____

_____

_____

_____

_____

_____

• Do you have any feelings or pictures about your personal growth that you want to change? If so, what are they?

_____

_____

_____

_____

_____

_____

_____

_____

_____

• Assume you have changed these feelings or pictures. Describe how you feel and what pictures you have as a result of the change.

_____

_____

_____

_____

_____

_____

_____

_____

_____

CREATING IMAGES ABOUT YOUR FINANCES

- Imagine yourself satisfying all of your financial needs. How do you feel?

_____

_____

_____

_____

_____

_____

_____

_____

_____

- Describe how you see yourself when you have the financial condition you want. Be as precise as possible.

_____

_____

_____

_____

_____

_____

_____

_____

_____

• Do you have any feelings or pictures about your finances that you want to change? If so, what are they?

_____

_____

_____

_____

_____

_____

_____

_____

_____

• Assume you have changed these feelings or pictures. Describe how you feel and what pictures you have as a result of the change.

_____

_____

_____

_____

_____

_____

_____

_____

_____

• Imagine yourself satisfying all of your career needs. How do you feel?

_____

_____

_____

_____

_____

_____

_____

_____

_____

• Describe how you see yourself when you have the career you want. Be as precise as possible.

_____

_____

_____

_____

_____

_____

_____

_____

_____

• Do you have any feelings or pictures about your career that you want to change? If so, what are they?

_____

_____

_____

_____

_____

_____

_____

_____

_____

_____

• Assume you have changed these feelings or pictures. Describe how you feel and what pictures you have as a result of the change.

_____

_____

_____

_____

_____

_____

_____

_____

_____

Goals

Achieving your goals is the primary purpose of the *Charting Your Goals* method. Goals state what you want to do or achieve. They satisfy your needs and wants and are your objectives or those things toward which you aim your attention.

There is a high degree of frustration associated with failure. It is important, therefore, that you set attainable goals. Ensuring that your goals are attainable means that they must be:

- **Achievable**

  Achievable goals are those you expect to succeed. Some goals require more commitment to attain than others. You should ensure that the undertaking necessary to achieve your goals is not beyond your willingness or ability. For example, if you want an advanced degree you need to be willing to accept the educational, financial, and time demands associated with the years of study that such a degree will require. Or, if you want to lose 20 pounds, you need to be willing to go on a diet and improve your level of exercise.

- **Satisfying**

  How you feel about yourself is important. Satisfying goals make you feel good about yourself. The more you feel good about yourself the more receptive you are to new ideas and opportunities. Choose goals that enhance your vitality, joy, and sense of peace. If you perceive that achieving a goal may require pain or sacrifice, aim toward a level of pain or sacrifice which is acceptable to you and reward yourself along the way.

In the following exercises you will have the opportunity to identify and state your goals. Throughout this process remember your values, needs, and wants.

Since goals focus on "what" rather than on "how," do not concern yourself with the means you will use to accomplish your goals. That step comes later. You will know your goals because they answer one or both of the following questions:

- "What do I need?"
- "What do I want?"

Again, do not confuse these questions with "How do I get what I need or want?"

Here are some examples.

For health:

- "I need to have more energy and feel better."
- "I want to look more trim and fit."

For career:

- "I need to have a more satisfying and better-paying job."
- "I want a career that gives me more free time."

For finances:

- "I want to make a million dollars this year."
- "I need to set up a trust fund for my kids' education."

For relationships:

- "I need to have a more satisfying relationship with my life partner."
- "I want to be more well liked and respected by my peers."

For personal growth:

- "I want to be happier."
- "I need to improve my level of education."

You will notice that goal statements make frequent use of comparative adjectives. If you wish, you may also add time frames to your goals. Remember, however, the information about time in chapter 1 and be flexible.

What are your health goals? Describe each goal in detail using complete sentences, i.e., "I need . . ." or "I want . . ."

*   _____

    _____

*   _____

    _____

*   _____

    _____

*   _____

    _____

*   _____

    _____

*   _____

    _____

*   _____

    _____

*   _____

    _____

*   _____

    _____

*   _____

    _____

What are your relationship goals? Describe each goal in detail using complete sentences, i.e., "I need . . ." or "I want . . ."

- _____
  _____

- _____
  _____

- _____
  _____

- _____
  _____

- _____
  _____

- _____
  _____

- _____
  _____

- _____
  _____

- _____
  _____

- _____
  _____

What are your personal growth goals? Describe each goal in detail using complete sentences, i.e., "I need . . ." or "I want . . ."

*   _____
    _____

*   _____
    _____

*   _____
    _____

*   _____
    _____

*   _____
    _____

*   _____
    _____

*   _____
    _____

*   _____
    _____

*   _____
    _____

*   _____
    _____

What are your financial goals? Describe each goal in detail using complete sentences, i.e., "I need . . ." or "I want . . ."

- _____

  _____

- _____

  _____

- _____

  _____

- _____

  _____

- _____

  _____

- _____

  _____

- _____

  _____

- _____

  _____

- _____

  _____

What are your career goals? Describe each goal in detail using complete sentences, i.e., "I need . . ." or "I want . . ."

- _____
  _____

- _____
  _____

- _____
  _____

- _____
  _____

- _____
  _____

- _____
  _____

- _____
  _____

- _____
  _____

- _____
  _____

- _____
  _____

Strategies and Tactics

Once you have set your goals, you need to determine how you will achieve them. What means are at your disposal for attaining success? You need to have a plan. Planning is allocating resources according to a strategy. Your resources include your time, intelligence, assets, and energy. Your plan is your way of arranging those resources most effectively for achieving your goals. The way you arrange them becomes your strategy.

The word *strategy* comes from the Greek word meaning "generalship" and is a method for accomplishing one's objectives. Strategy may also be viewed as the art of gaining advantage through a plan.

Most people recognize that there are a number of ways of achieving each goal. Some are more easily attained than others. The strategy you adopt is the way you decide to achieve a particular goal or, perhaps, several goals. It is the plan you create based on what you perceive to be the optimal way to achieve results.

Strategies should be used as long as they work. If a particular strategy does not achieve the intended goal within a reasonable time frame, you should consider adopting another. Therefore, when developing a strategy it is important to be flexible. One strategy may be better than another but may also carry greater risks. For example, if you want a career that is more satisfying and gives you more control over your time, you may consider setting up your own business rather than looking for a position with an established firm. That strategy may be perfect for your circumstances and carries with it risks about having enough capital in reserve and building a strong enough network to sustain you until your business generates the level of income you need to maintain your lifestyle.

You should be discriminating when choosing one strategy over another. This is particularly true when one or more of your strategies overlap or are somehow interdependent.

Circumstances sometimes change the usefulness of one strategy when compared with another. When opportunities or obstacles (which may or may not have been anticipated) present themselves, you should be prepared to revise your strategy, if appropriate. In that sense, quick thinking and easy wit are good sailing companions.

Building on several examples of goals shown in the preceding section, some strategies might include the following:

Goal	"I need to have more energy and feel better."
Strategy	"Consult my physician about my health concerns."
Strategy	"Begin a diet and physical fitness program."
Goal	"I want to have a more satisfying and better-paying job."
Strategy	"Initiate a search for job offers."
Strategy	"Attend professional gatherings to extend my career network."

Goal	"I need to have a more satisfying relationship with my life partner."
Strategy	"Allow more private time for the two of us."
Strategy	"Do something special for my partner each week."

Putting your strategies into action is the next step. Strategies are executed by a series of tactics.

Tactic, also from a Greek word, means the arrangement of your plan so that it is ready for immediate action. Tactics, therefore, are the individual steps that must be taken to implement your strategy.

To determine your tactics, divide your strategy into each of the "action items" that you will need to perform. It is a good idea to think of tactics as those things you can do today or in the near future which will advance you one step or several steps closer to your goal.

Here are some examples.

Goal	"I need to have more energy and feel better."
Strategy	"Consult my physician about my health concerns."
Tactic	"Write down each of my health concerns."
Tactic	"Call my doctor for an appointment."

Goal	"I want to have a more satisfying and better-paying job."
Strategy	"Initiate a search for job offers."
Tactic	"Update my resume."
Tactic	"Contact a professional job counselor."
Tactic	"Look through the job postings at work and in the newspaper."
Tactic	"Telephone two of my colleagues about possible openings in their firms."

You may have more than one strategy for each goal and more than one tactic for each strategy. Similarly, one strategy may serve more than one goal and one tactic may assist more than one strategy.

On the following pages summarize each goal that you established in the preceding section. Write it in the appropriate place and identify the strategy or strategies you will use to accomplish it. Also list the tactics you will employ to execute each strategy.

For each of your health goals, describe the strategy or strategies you will use to achieve the goal and what tactics you will employ.

Goals	Strategies
	Tactics

Goals	Strategies
	Tactics

Goals	Strategies
	Tactics

Goals	Strategies
	Tactics

Goals	Strategies
	Tactics

For each of your relationship goals, describe the strategy or strategies you will use to achieve the goal and what tactics you will employ.

Goals	Strategies
	Tactics

Goals	Strategies
	Tactics

Goals	Strategies
	Tactics

Goals	Strategies
	Tactics

Goals	Strategies
	Tactics

— PLANNING STRATEGIES AND TACTICS FOR YOUR PERSONAL GROWTH GOALS —

For each of your personal growth goals, describe the strategy or strategies you will use to achieve the goal and what tactics you will employ.

Goals	Strategies
	Tactics

Goals	Strategies
	Tactics

Goals	Strategies
	Tactics

Goals	Strategies
	Tactics

Goals	Strategies
	Tactics

For each of your financial goals, describe the strategy or strategies you will use to achieve the goal and what tactics you will employ.

Goals	Strategies
	Tactics

Goals

Strategies

Tactics

Goals	Strategies
	Tactics

Goals	Strategies
	Tactics

Goals

Strategies

Tactics

For each of your career goals, describe the strategy or strategies you will use to achieve the goal and what tactics you will employ.

Goals	Strategies
	Tactics

Goals

Strategies

Tactics

Goals	Strategies
	Tactics

Goals	Strategies
	Tactics

Goals	Strategies
	Tactics

Making Your Charts

The *Charting Your Goals* charts are a map or pictorial representation of everything that is important to you about each goal area. Having completed the previous exercises you now have nearly all of the components you need to make your charts. You will find one each for your health, relationship, personal growth, career, and financial goals on the following pages.

There are two ways you may want to fill in the charts:

- **Creatively**

  Your first pass at filling in the charts should call upon your creativity. Brainstorm. Let your first thoughts out. If you have an image about your health, for example, or a need or a goal that comes to mind related to your health, write it down. Write what you think spontaneously. This approach relies upon intuition. Editing your thoughts before they are put on paper impedes the creative process.

- **Logically**

  Once you have written down your creative thoughts, think through each of the categories for any idea you recorded. For example, if you have a goal about your finances, think about the values you have relating to financial matters and describe the needs and wants that stem from those values. Write down the images that come to mind about achieving your goal and about your satisfaction at having your underlying needs and wants met. Next think through and commit to paper what the best strategy or strategies for you to achieve your goal may be, and then list the tactics you will need to execute to make your strategy or strategies successful.

This is a comprehensive approach to developing your life goals. You should work comfortably at your own pace. There is no "rule" that you have to start with a "goal" or your "values." What is important is that you have the whole picture. What comes to mind may be a strategy or a tactic or an image. Write it down and then go back and fill in the other areas. If you start with the strategy of losing 20 pounds, for example, what is the goal you have in mind? What image do you have? What tactics will you execute in the near future? What are the needs and wants you have that bring this strategy to mind? What values do you hold? Also, refer to the sample charts, beginning on page 56.

CHARTING YOUR GOALS

Values	

Needs	Images
Wants	

Commitments

Goals

Strategies

Tactics

CHARTING YOUR GOALS

Values

Needs

Images

Wants

Commitments

Goals

Strategies

Tactics

CHARTING YOUR GOALS

Values

Needs	Images
Wants	

Commitments

Goals

Strategies

Tactics

CHARTING YOUR GOALS

Values

Needs

Images

Wants

Commitments

Goals

Strategies

Tactics

CHARTING YOUR GOALS

Values	
Needs	**Images**
Wants	

Commitments

Goals

Strategies

Tactics

four
COMMITMENT

This chapter addresses:

- How an optimistic frame of mind influences your images and, in turn, how your images can be used to change your frame of mind.
- How to have courage in the face of obstacles and stress.
- How making commitments is the basis for an optimistic frame of mind.
- How to maintain the momentum generated during the *Charting Your Goals* program.

Your work with the *Charting Your Goals* program has introduced you to the essential tools for setting your personal life-goals and for establishing the strategies and tactics you need to achieve them. The remaining key ingredient is commitment.

Making Commitments

A commitment is an agreement or pledge to do something in the future. It is your contract with yourself to do what is necessary to achieve your goals. Your commitment to execute the tactics necessary to ensure that your strategies are given the opportunity to be successful is a prerequisite to achieving your goals.

The by-product of commitment is courage and momentum. When you make the commitment to reach your goals you will have the courage to face obstacles and maintain the course you have set for yourself. **Commitment is an ongoing process.**

Some commitments are easy to make and keep; others may be quite difficult. One commitment may require a degree of sacrifice, such as a commitment relating to diets and losing weight. Another commitment may be more pleasurable, such as one to take a special vacation.

The *Charting Your Goals* method has thus far assisted you in identifying goals in key areas of your life. You have developed one or more strategies for reaching each of these goals and know the tactics you could take today or in the near future to bring you closer to your objectives. You must now make a commitment and proceed. Your reward for being committed to achieving your goals is having them materialize and experiencing the happiness and satisfaction that comes with success.

The form of your commitment should be a positive declaration of your intention to follow the strategies and execute the tactics you have developed; for example, "I pledge to take all steps I have documented to reach my financial goals," or "I promise to do everything necessary to reach my health goals," or "I commit myself to executing my career strategies and tactics." Whatever your commitment says, you should consider it a binding agreement with yourself which you will faithfully pursue until you reach or, perhaps, modify your goals.

In the following section, develop your own Declaration of Commitment.

——————— DECLARATION OF COMMITMENT ———————

Compose your own sentence or paragraph which states your pledge to:

- Follow the strategies you have established.
- Execute the tactics you have decided upon for today and the near future.
- Reach your goals.

Commitments need to be renewed frequently. There is always a ready reason for not doing what you said you would do. Use the Declaration of Commitment you have composed frequently as an affirmation. Write it at the top of each of your charts. You may choose to make a single statement in conjunction with all of your goals, or multiple statements particular to individual goals.

Courage, Obstacles, and Stress

Every successful voyage includes some measure of adventure and, often, unexpected obstacles. You may experience obstacles which impede your success, as well as frustration when your goals do not materialize when or how you planned.

There are essentially two types of obstacles:

- **Those which you place in your path**
  These are your way of telling yourself that you are not ready to achieve a particular goal, or that you are not sure you want to achieve the goal you have set. Often these obstacles materialize as some mode of self-sabotage. Not studying for an important examination, eating things which are not on your diet, and habitually arriving for work late are some examples of ways in which people may be setting themselves up for failure.

- **Those which others place in your path**
  There are a number of reasons why people place obstacles in the path of another. Sometimes it is out of jealousy, sometimes out of concern, and sometimes out of ignorance. A co-worker may undercut you on an important assignment by failing to give you some critical data, a parent may withhold approbation in the hope of changing a child's decision, and a friend may change plans that he did not realize were critical to your own activities. In all cases, these obstacles appear to be out of your control.

It is easy to perceive yourself as the victim of either type of obstacle. You may lay blame for your own sabotage on a circumstance, a feeling, or an illness. You may lay blame for the sabotage of others on one or more of many factors. The point which is important to recognize is that sabotage does not occur in a vacuum. Somehow you managed to create or attract it and, in that sense, you are responsible for its effects.

It takes courage to face these obstacles because they are telling you something important about your goals. It is something that, until you confronted the obstacle, you were either not willing to look at or not conscious of; for example, the need to set another goal, to negotiate for someone else's support, or to renew your commitment to reaching the goal.

Courage is the strength to persevere and to withstand the obstacle you are facing. Courage has both mental and moral aspects. It is both the conviction that you are able to remain resolute in your undertaking, and the ability to take action in the face of difficulty or even danger. The Taoists speak of courage stemming from internal balance. In a life-planning context, it is necessary to maintain balance between the many forces required to bring success to your endeavors.

Failure to achieve your goals because of obstacles is frequently accompanied by stress. Stress is the effect on the body of mental tension. If left unchecked, stress may result in illness. Managing stress is a necessary component of ensuring a successful life-plan.

There are many means to transform stress and limit its negative impact on your success and health. These include the proper amount of physical exercise and the practice of meditation or relaxation, as well as specialized techniques which are well documented by stress management specialists. You should become aware of a way of managing stress that works for you and practice it regularly.

When obstacles are persistent, generally speaking, continued exertion will not further your achievement. In fact, it may add to whatever stress you may be experiencing. Persevering failure may be a signal that your goal is unrealistic. You may need to review your tactics and time frames. Or, circumstances may have changed more quickly than you or your environment are able to handle. Too much stress is a signal that you need to pause and take another look at your goal.

Optimism

Being committed to do what is necessary to achieve your goals gives you a sense of hope about the future and is the basis for an optimistic frame of mind.

Optimism is derived from the Latin word meaning "best." It is an inclination to anticipate the most favorable outcome of events. When you deliberately assume an optimistic attitude in your thoughts, your words and actions will reflect this state of mind. You develop a greater sense of the positive and begin to operate as if this is the best of all possible worlds, now is the best of all possible times, and what you want is the best of all possible things to have.

You may say that such statements do not reflect the reality in which you live. Remember, however, that reaching your goals will change your present reality and open up new avenues of opportunity to you. When you set forth plans laid in self-doubt and fear of failure, your actions reflect those negative trends and your probability of success diminishes. When you choose to be optimistic, however, your plans are nourished and your probability of success is enhanced.

There are three ways to create optimism:

- **Approach your goals with an image of your success.**
  Paint vivid mental pictures of yourself being successful and achieving your goals. Create images of you fulfilling your health, relationship, personal growth, financial, and career goals. Use metaphors that speak of success in present tense; for example, "I am now earning $50,000 per year."

- **Doubt your doubts.**
  You may have many doubts about your eventual success. Most people do. However, your doubts have no more significance than any other random thought you may have. By doubting your doubts you focus your attention on positive thoughts about achieving your goals. You take away the power that most people give to the doubts they have. This enhances your receptivity to whatever goal you may want to achieve.

- **Radiate success.**

  Be that which you would seem. This Indian proverb admonishes you to live as if you are the success you want to be. Radiating success in your thoughts, words, and deeds is a declaration to yourself and others that you are a winner and that you expect achievement.

Imaging and Your Frame of Mind

In chapter 1, you examined how your attitudes are greatly influenced by your viewpoints. In making day-to-day choices you may find yourself highly disposed to undertake certain actions and to refrain from other activities based on your frame of mind or feelings about the perceived outcome. You are more likely to do something if your attitude about it is positive.

In *Charting Your Goals,* you began to look at key viewpoints—those concerning time, money, power, failure, success, and process—as a means of observing yourself. You may have realized that your viewpoints are complex images you create to assist you in describing your life and managing the sensory and intellectual information you receive each day. Most viewpoints operate on the subconscious level. That simply means that you are not always consciously aware of your viewpoints or of how they might influence you as you go about your daily activities.

Most often, people become aware of their viewpoints when something changes. Receiving an unexpected bit of news or traveling to an unfamiliar place can bring about new ways of thinking about something which may have been routine. You find that your current viewpoints may not serve changed circumstances or interests.

Viewpoints tend to remain constant until consciously altered. You experience many examples of your viewpoints at work each day:

- What you eat is influenced by the preferences you have developed for certain tastes and, perhaps, by perceptions you have about good nutrition.
- The kind of work you do is based on your education and career interests.
- The leisure activities in which you engage are those you find relaxing and pleasurable.

Your viewpoints are the result of the many choices you have made in the past, the suggestions you may have received from others, and also the successes and failures you have experienced over time.

In becoming more aware of your feelings and frame of mind, you will also come to realize that, as you change your viewpoint, your attitudes begin to shift. This realization gives you a very powerful tool for life-planning and achieving your goals: you can change your attitudes by changing your viewpoint.

Changing your viewpoint about a specific topic is a two-step process:

- **Become aware of your viewpoint.**
  As you observe yourself, become conscious of the values and current images you have about a particular topic or viewpoint. Look at your present images and the metaphors you use in describing this viewpoint.

- **Create a new image.**
  Decide how you want your current image to change and, in your mind's eye, visualize a new image. As this new image becomes stronger, it will begin to influence your viewpoint and change your attitude about it.

The ability to manage your frame of mind through this process allows you to expand the opportunities you have for success because it allows you the freedom to remain optimistic in the face of obstacles and stress.

CREATING AN OPTIMISTIC VIEWPOINT

In order to demonstrate how you can create an optimistic viewpoint, do the following exercise.

Make yourself comfortable and relax. Recall a situation where you had doubts about your ability to succeed. Once you have pictured that circumstance:

- Think about a positive incident from your childhood, one where things went well for you.
- Place yourself in that picture now.
- What are your feelings about this positive situation? Recognize where in your body these feelings are located and put your attention on that place.
- Close your eyes, relax, and take a few deep breaths. Let yourself experience your positive feelings.

When you recall the original picture again remember the positive feelings in your body and create a positive association to overlay your doubts.

Treat each obstacle in the same manner. Create an alternative positive image and let the new image overlay the old.

As you go through this process you will observe new feelings and have a changed awareness about your old viewpoints. Let go of those feelings, thoughts, and doubts that place limits on your ability to succeed. Replace them with affirmations and optimistic images consistent with your new realizations.

Maintaining Momentum

You are well on your way to success. Doing the *Charting Your Goals* exercises has given you the impetus to make headway on your lifelong voyage to satisfy your goals.

In order to maintain this momentum there are three things you can do:

- Keep your charts visible. Refer to them often and use them as a daily reference.
- Keep a list of tactics you plan on executing and update it each day, crossing off those you have completed and adding any additional ones that may occur to you.
- Set aside several hours every 30 days to checkpoint where you are on your voyage. Make any adjustments in your course that are appropriate for your current circumstances. Modify your strategies or renew your commitments, as appropriate.

Keep your courage up, live a long life, and be healthy, happy, and prosperous in all of your adventures.

EXTRA CHARTS

CHARTING YOUR GOALS

Values

Needs

Images

Wants

Commitments	
Goals	**Strategies**
	Tactics

CHARTING YOUR GOALS

Values

Needs	Images

Wants	

132

Commitments	
Goals	**Strategies**
	Tactics

CHARTING YOUR GOALS

Values

Needs	Images

Wants	

Commitments	
Goals	**Strategies**
	Tactics

CHARTING YOUR GOALS

Values	
Needs	**Images**
Wants	

Commitments	
Goals	**Strategies**
	Tactics

CHARTING YOUR GOALS

Values	
Needs	**Images**
Wants	

Commitments	
Goals	**Strategies**
	Tactics

CHARTING YOUR GOALS

Values

Needs	Images

Wants	

Commitments	
Goals	**Strategies**
	Tactics

CHARTING YOUR GOALS

Values

Needs

Images

Wants

Commitments

Goals	Strategies
	Tactics

CHARTING YOUR GOALS

Values

Needs

Images

Wants

Commitments

Goals

Strategies

Tactics

CHARTING YOUR GOALS

Values

Needs

Images

Wants

Commitments	
Goals	**Strategies**
	Tactics

CHARTING YOUR GOALS

Values

Needs

Images

Wants

Commitments	
Goals	**Strategies**
	Tactics

149

CHARTING YOUR GOALS

Values

Needs	Images
Wants	

Commitments	
Goals	**Strategies**
	Tactics

CHARTING YOUR GOALS

Values

Needs	Images

Wants	

Commitments

Goals

Strategies

Tactics

CHARTING YOUR GOALS

Values

Needs

Images

Wants

Commitments	
Goals	**Strategies**
	Tactics

CHARTING YOUR GOALS

Values

Needs	Images
Wants	

Commitments

Goals

Strategies

Tactics

INDEX